of related interest

A Beginner's Guide to Autism Spectrum Disorders
Essential Information for Parents and Professionals
Paul G. Taylor
ISBN 978 1 84905 233 7

Can I tell you about Asperger Syndrome?
A guide for friends and family
Jude Welton
ISBN 978 1 84310 206 9

The ASD Workbook
Understanding Your Autism Spectrum Disorder
Penny Kershaw
ISBN 978 1 84905 195 8

Autism All-Stars
How We Use Our Autism and Asperger Traits to Shine in Life
Edited by Josie Santomauro
ISBN 978 1 84310 188 8

Raising Martians – from Crash-landing to Leaving Home
How to Help a Child with Asperger Syndrome or High-functioning Autism
Joshua Muggleton
ISBN 978 1 84905 002 9

Asperger Syndrome – What Teachers Need to Know
Second Edition
Matt Winter with Clare Lawrence
ISBN 978 1 84905 203 0

Embracing Asperger's
A Primer for Parents and Professionals
Richard Bromfield, PhD
ISBN 978 1 84905 818 6

Finding Out about Asperger's Syndrome, High Functioning Autism and PDD

Gunilla Gerland

Jessica Kingsley *Publishers*
London and Philadelphia

Acknowledgements
The illustrations on pages 9 and 11 are reproduced by kind permission of Gunilla Gerland and Bokförlaget Cura and the illustration on page 25 is reproduced courtesy of Annika Almberg and Bokförlaget Cura. The photograph of Hans Asperger on page 43 is reproduced by kind permission of Läkartidningen and Chistopher Gillberg.

First published in 1997 in Sweden by Bokförlaget Cura AB
English edition published in 2000 by
Jessica Kingsley Publishers Ltd
116 Pentonville Road
London N1 9JB, England
and
400 Market Street, Suite 400
Philadelphia, PA 19106 USA

www.jkp.com

Library of Congress Cataloging in Publication Data

Gerland, Gunilla.
Finding out about asperger syndrome, high-functioning autism and PDD / Gunilla Gerland.
p. cm.
ISBN 1 85302 840 1 (alk. paper)
1. Asperger's syndrome Popular works. I. Title.
RC553.A88G47 1999 99-40289
616.89'82-dc21 CIP

British Library Cataloguing in Publication Data
A CIP catalogue record for this book is available from the British Library

ISBN 978 1 85302 840 3
eISBN 978 0 85700 146 7

Contents

You and me
and Asperger's syndrome

Perhaps you have just learned that you or someone you know has Asperger's syndrome or autism.

Asperger's syndrome and autism are disabilities, and they're a bit unusual since you can't see them on the outside. This sometimes makes it hard for other people to understand that you have difficulties. So you may need to explain to them that you have a disability. When you're explaining, it will help if you yourself know what it is. It also helps if you have a book that you and others can read. That's why I've written this book.

A young man with Asperger's syndrome once described how he feels when things are difficult: 'Everything goes in all directions'. I think it describes the feeling very well.

I, the author of this book, have high-functioning autism. Asperger's syndrome is a form of autism, and so is PDD (pervasive developmental disorder). Some people think that Asperger's syndrome and high functioning autism are the same thing. Therefore I will sometimes write 'Asperger's syndrome' and sometimes 'autism' in this book. (Although I won't actually use the term 'PDD' I am including it when I write about autism.)

Autism and Asperger's syndrome aren't exactly the same in all of us who have it. So you may not recognize everything in this book.

The young man I mentioned before, who talked about things going in all directions, also said that when he feels good everything is sort of flowing in the same direction.

What are our difficulties?

Motor skills

The ways the brain steers the body's movements are known as 'motor skills'. Some of us with autism have problems with our motor skills. We may seem clumsy. We may walk or talk differently.

For instance, I used to spill things a lot when I was younger. I wasn't good at PE in school either.

Thinking differently

When you have Asperger's syndrome it usually means you think differently, though it's hard to describe in what way. A different way of thinking may lead to many misunderstandings. It can also lead to fights and make other people angry.

But a different way of thinking can also be an advantage: you may come up with something nobody ever thought of before.

Some famous people are believed to have had autism or Asperger's syndrome, although they never got one of those diagnoses since autism wasn't known at the time they lived. Albert Einstein is one of them.

Albert Einstein's field of work was physics. At the end of the nineteenth century science had very firm ideas about the laws of physics. Einstein could think differently and come up with things that no one had yet understood. He worked by making thought experiments and he became very famous due to his discoveries about the laws of physics.

It's usually a good idea to ask!

Since many misunderstandings may arise if you have Asperger's syndrome or autism it can be very helpful if there's someone you can ask.

The difficulties you have may be different when you are different ages. Now that I'm a grown-up the hardest thing for me is that I have to think so much to get things right. As a result some things take me a very long time to do. I also find it hard to know how to act around other people.

One student with Asperger's syndrome said: 'It's good when the teachers in school know a lot about autism. Then you can ask if something goes wrong or you don't understand.'

If you know someone with autism or Asperger's syndrome it's also a good idea to ask how he or she likes things.

Sometimes people try to figure out how I want things to be without asking me. Sometimes they forget that I am different from them and they get it all wrong. That's why it's always best if they ask me.

Our five senses

Human beings have five senses: the sense of smell, sight, hearing, taste and touch. Almost everybody with autism and Asperger's syndrome has problems with some of their senses.

The experience with any one sense – for example, the experience of touch – can be very different for you to the experiences of other people. This may make you feel uncomfortable and you may not want anybody to touch you. You may not want to wear certain clothes.

I had problems with other people touching me when I was younger. It hurt if people just touched me lightly. They sometimes said to me that it couldn't hurt. In fact, it did hurt because my sense of touch was different.

If you have autism you may also have difficulty keeping apart all the information you get from your senses. This means that many people or a lot of noise may be very overwhelming and difficult to handle. For some of us, it's just certain sounds – or maybe smells – which are difficult.

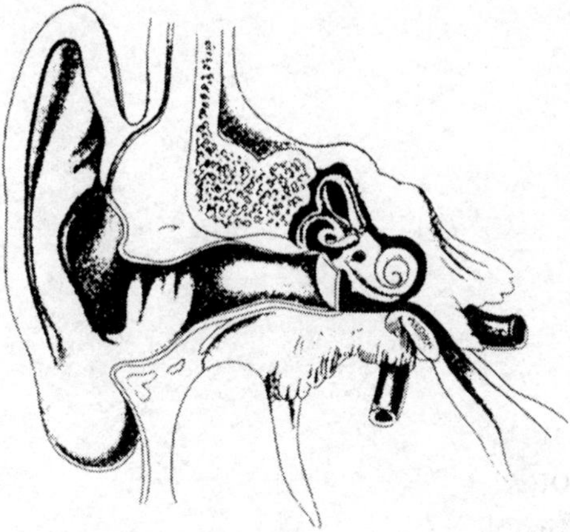

Hearing is one of our five senses.

But we don't just have difficulties…

Having autism or Asperger's syndrome doesn't just mean that you have difficulties. We usually have a special interest: something we're extremely good at, or know a lot about.

Many people with Asperger's syndrome who I've met think it's an advantage to know a lot about something or to like doing something very much. But sometimes you may need help from other people to learn how to make time for other things too.

People with autism or Asperger's syndrome have many talents. For instance, many of us are very orderly. We do a job thoroughly, and we finish what we start.

Other people sometimes think it's a problem that I always want to finish what I'm doing, or do just one thing at a time. But I think other people are often very careless, both in what they say and what they do. For instance, they don't always finish off what they're doing.

If you have Asperger's syndrome maybe you want to stop and think about what your difficulties are. And what your strengths are.

What Asperger's Syndrome is to me

Learning that you have a disability

I've talked to several people about how they felt when they learned that they had autism or Asperger's syndrome. They have told me different things. Some became very sad. Others thought it was a relief to learn why they were different as they had already noticed they were so. Some felt both good and bad at the same time when they learned about the diagnosis.

One person with Asperger's syndrome told me he felt cheated because when he was younger he had asked others if he was disabled, and they had said he wasn't. But he said he felt that it was better to know about it anyway.

When I was younger I didn't know I had autism. I often felt that I must be weird or stupid, and I really tried hard to be like everybody else.

If you feel like I did when you were told you have autism or Asperger's syndrome, you may think that this means that other people have a right to think that you are weird. You may become very sad and maybe you won't want to hear anything about the diagnosis.

It's a pity if you do think like this. Having Asperger's syndrome doesn't means that you are weird – it just means that you are different. And it doesn't mean that other people are right and that you are wrong.

Why is it called Asperger's syndrome?

Asperger's Syndrome got its name from a doctor named Hans Asperger who first described this disability. It is said that he also had some traits of Asperger's syndrome.

When do you get Asperger's syndrome?

People believe that you are either born with Asperger's syndrome or you get it in early childhood.

Hans Asperger was born in 1906 and died in 1980. He worked as a doctor in Austria and studied a group of children (mostly boys) who had what now is called Asperger's syndrome. Hans Asperger was probably the first person to understand that this disability had advantages as well as disadvantages.

How do you get Asperger's syndrome?

Many researchers are trying to find the cause of Asperger's syndrome and autism and they think it has several different causes. Sometimes Asperger's syndrome is hereditary, so you may have relatives with Asperger's syndrome or autism. It can also be caused by a mother catching an infection during pregnancy which affects the baby before birth.

Some final words

Finally, I want to say to those of you who have Asperger's syndrome: be proud of who you are. You have the right to be yourself, and other people should accept you as you are.

And to those of you who know someone with Asperger's syndrome: respect his or her disability and don't try to change this person. It can be exciting to get to know somebody who isn't like everybody else.

And to all: Being different is just as good as being like everyone else.

Lightning Source UK Ltd.
Milton Keynes UK
UKOW021413201211

184131UK00001B/9/P

9 781853 02840